CW00539495

Thirteenth-century Conwy Castle and the medieval town sit on the River Conwy's spectacular estuary.

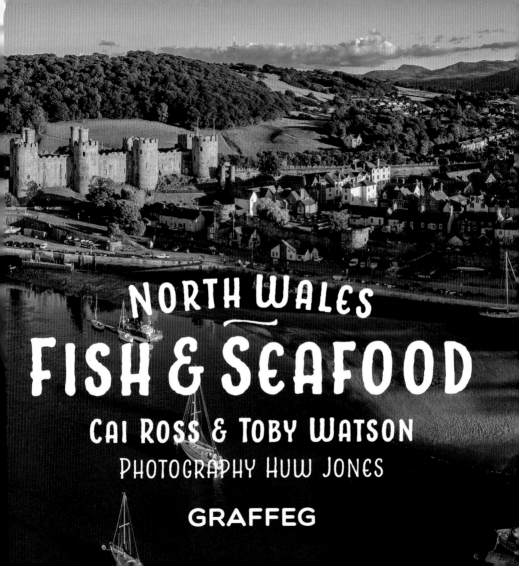

NORTH WALES
FISH & SEAFOOD

CAI ROSS & TOBY WATSON

PHOTOGRAPHY HUW JONES

GRAFFEG

CONTENTS

CAI ROSS: MY NORTH WALES

Sometimes you have to go away and come back to realise how lucky you were in the first place. I had lived in North Wales for my whole life and, being young and foolish, had scarcely noticed that I was going about my daily business in an area of extraordinary natural beauty.

I had been living for a while in London and returned to our house in Deganwy for the summer. One morning I opened my eyes and the first thing that I saw was the view across the ship-dotted water: Conwy Castle, its Telford-designed bridge reaching out away from me to the left, flanked on its right by the fishing town of Conwy itself, forests, trees and Mynydd y Dref rising above it all, with the misty peaks of Eryri visible in the distance.

All of this was framed inside the open window of the bedroom like a widescreen still from a Technicolor David Lean film about trawlermen in the nineteenth century. It was even sunny! It was one of the most intoxicating, overpoweringly beautiful things that I'd ever seen, and

I had to remind myself that this had actually been the view from my house since I was a teenager.

I was reminded of that moment during the coronavirus lockdown, when holidays to far-flung areas of the world suddenly became day trips to places within your own county. We discovered dozens of soul-enriching walks and treks from testing ascents to breezy coastal ambles. Everywhere we went, we'd nod politely at passers-by (from a respectable distance, of course) and every time the same comment: 'Lucky to have this on our doorstep, aren't we?'

North Wales has been my doorstep since day one. I was born in the Denbighshire market town of Ruthin and spent my first eight years on a hill farm in nearby Cyffylliog, playing fast and loose with Health and Safety rules by building dens inside vast stacks of hay bales. We moved to a village near Corwen in 1983 when my Dad, ignoring his wiser, more sensible instincts, bought and renovated an old pub, The Goat. My parents spent a gruelling five years running it before we packed up and headed to the coast.

Left: The Menai Strait separates the island of Anglesey from mainland Wales.

They opened Paysanne in 1988. My mum had always had a passion for the kind of French country-style cookery championed by Elizabeth David and after five years cooking chicken and chips (excellent chicken and chips, I might add) she wanted to take her skill-set up a few levels. Fortunately, a steadily increasing number of regulars were very glad that she did.

At that time, North Wales was not especially known as a Mecca for dazzling, innovative cuisine. That has now changed completely. Diverse tastes are catered for all over the area from ingenious Michelin-starred tasting menus to hearty pub lunches to fill the belly and the soul.

Simultaneously, North Wales had recently seen a sharp growth in the number of locally produced ales, spirits and even wines that have been winning bucketloads of international awards left, right and centre.

I suspect that in the past many people – like me – were rather unaware about the great culinary treasures that had been all around them, staring them in the face the whole time. Free-range meats, lambs gorged on sweeping grasslands, 250 miles of coastline studded with all the core ingredients for a majestic platter of *fruits de mer*.

Some chefs, like Ellis and Liam Barrie, who returned to the site of their halcyon childhood holidays on Anglesey to set up the acclaimed, much-missed Marram Grass, spotted North Wales's foodie potential from afar. Others, like renowned chef Bryn Williams, were born and raised here and never doubted that they were surrounded on all sides by delectable ingredients in abundance.

After several years of renewal, I truly believe that North Wales can hold its own as one of the great natural chef's larders, up there with anywhere else in the UK. Moreover, an influx of new tourist-attracting developments has capitalised on the area's immense popularity with fans of the outdoors, including the longest zip wire in Europe. Ever fancied playing golf in an underground cavern? We have that too!

Right: Specials board showing the variety of fresh produce from Mermaid Seafoods, Llandudno.

1984

FOOD

SPECIALS

(LOCAL WILD (SEABASS)
WHOLE & FILLETED)

6/8
WILD CAUGHT
WHOLE PRAWNS
£23.50 BOX.

SEA
B
£3
(TAK
OU
S

YOUNGS FISHFINGERS
60 PER PACK
£8.50.

WHOLE
SARDINES.

POUSSINS
£3.00 EACH

CATCH OF THE DA

COD CHEEKS

Sonya

With the greatest collection of preserved medieval castles in the UK, the mountainous beauty of Eryri and the unique citadel to inspired eccentricity that is Portmeirion, North Wales has of late been singled out for its breathtaking outdoor splendour, making it a prized destination for walkers, climbers, surfers and bog-snorkelers from all over the world. A famous travel guide recently ranked North Wales as the fourth best region to visit in the world! As countless guests at Paysanne have told me, 'This is Zealand... just minus the 24-hour plane journey.'

I took over Paysanne from my parents in 2003 when they retired. When I came back to Deganwy there was a new kid in town. Toby Watson had set up his own restaurant, Sands, just up the road from Paysanne. Toby is one of the very best chefs in North Wales. He now caters for clients like Formula 1 teams and the occasional HRH and feeds thousands of wedding guests every year.

He and I have both decided that it's about time North Wales had its very own seafood cookbook. Not just your basic, average, everyday, ordinary, run-of-the-mill, ho-hum seafood cookbook either, but a celebration of the area's unique status as a banquet for all the senses, especially taste. Here you will discover sights to leave you breathless and recipes to get your taste buds ringing like fire alarms.

We'll be tipping our hats to the seafood heroes of North Wales who have poured their hearts and souls into their proud endeavours and have helped to create a unique area of outstanding natural bounty.

We're quite sure that by the end of this literary gastronomic journey, you'll understand just why 'Lucky to have this on our doorstep, aren't we?' became such a mantra in those dark days of lockdown. You won't necessarily have to have authentic North Wales ingredients to do justice to your creations, but if you want the real deal, why not pay North Wales a visit? Just make sure you bring a shopping basket, a decent pair of walking boots and an appetite.

Cai Ross

Left: Cai Ross & Toby Watson.

SCALLOPS

Scallops offer a delicate and unique flavour, providing a delectable seafood experience whether seared, grilled, or incorporated into various dishes.

Combined with their versatility, quick cooking time and gourmet appeal, they make a delightful addition to your culinary repertoire.

- Scallops have a distinct, sweet and delicate flavour that sets them apart from other seafood options. Their taste, often described as buttery, makes them a favourite among seafood enthusiasts.

- A nutritious choice, scallops offer an excellent source of high-quality protein, are low in fat and contain important vitamins and minerals like vitamin B12, magnesium and potassium. They also provide omega-3 fatty acids, which are beneficial for heart health, and are relatively low in calories while still providing essential nutrients.

- Scallops are incredibly versatile and can be prepared in various ways: seared, grilled, baked, or even enjoyed raw in ceviche. Their minimal cooking time, typically just a few minutes on each side, makes them a convenient option for a fast and delicious meal.

- A frequent feature in high-end restaurants, scallops are often associated with gourmet cuisine and can add an elegant touch to your meals when enjoyed at home for a special occasion or a treat.

GWINLLAN VINEYARD, CONWY

In 2012, there wasn't a grape to be found in North Wales, save the occasional garnish on the cheeseboard of Colin and Charlotte Bennett, who were living there at the time. It had always been their dream to plant a vineyard there, and encouraged by the readouts of the soil compatibility in their fields, they set about doing just that.

'A lot of people thought we were genuinely insane,' remembers Colin, 'but four years later, we were harvesting our initial crop. By May 2016 Gwinllan Conwy was open for business, not just selling our wonderful wine but offering vineyard tours too.'

It takes more than just scattering grape seeds in a random field and crossing your fingers to get a vineyard up and running. All sorts of elements have to be in play, and Colin and Charlotte were in a much better position than they could have hoped for in their wildest dreams. Colin told me, 'What we didn't realise back then was that by good fortune, we'd settled on a unique piece of land that was absolutely perfect for growing vines.

'Vines love well-drained soil, and the shale slate composition of the land was perfect. The southerly sloping aspect of the vineyard, close to the sea, maximises sunshine and protects from late frosts. Add to this the special microclimate known as the Foehn Effect, which ensures an extended growing season, allowing the grapes to fully ripen.'

The result of all these near perfect conditions gives the vineyard a unique 'terroir' which inevitably led to the release of outstanding, award-winning wines, not just from early ripening hybrid varieties such as Solaris and Rondo, but beautiful wines from the classic varieties of Pinot Noir and Chardonnay!

'In fact, something like our limited release 2020 Chardonnay would be the perfect accompaniment to fish. Our cool climate enhances those classic Chardonnay flavours of citrus and apple which are then gently softened by the light maturing in American oak barrels.'

Colin and Charlotte's endeavours have seen them showered with trophies from some of the most prestigious wine awards in the world and even led to an invitation to 10 Downing Street.

It's quite a splendid feeling as a restaurateur to have wines on our *carte du vin*, nestled there amongst all the French varieties, which hail from literally five miles down the road. Their bone-dry Solaris white goes especially well with shellfish, particularly scallops.

Scallops are one of the ultimate seafood treats. In the waters off the coast of North Wales, the fishing of scallops is rigorously regulated and the use of seabed-churning dredgers is given short shrift in favour of far more sustainable hand-diving. The season for scallops in North Wales is pretty short too, but like lots of shellfish, they are farmed elsewhere and you can get hold of them most months of the year.

Versatile, unique, delicious. Food of the gods stuff. Now, a quick note on cooking scallops from Mr Watson...

'Not all scallops are created equal and to give specific cooking times is ultimately misleading, although a medium-large scallop will take two to three minutes on either side. When pan-frying scallops, they want to be as dry as possible, cooking with a small amount of oil and where necessary finished with butter. In a heavy-based frying pan with a high heat, sear the scallops on both sides to ensure a good colour. When using butter, add it in once a good colour has been achieved and spoon the butter over, allowing it to brown slightly, finishing with a squeeze of lemon. The scallops should still be soft to the touch without being bouncy.

To coral or not to coral? That is the question. Personally, I prefer to remove the coral and use it to make soups etc. Other people think that the coral is the best bit! I will leave the coral decision to you...'

www.gwinllan.co.uk

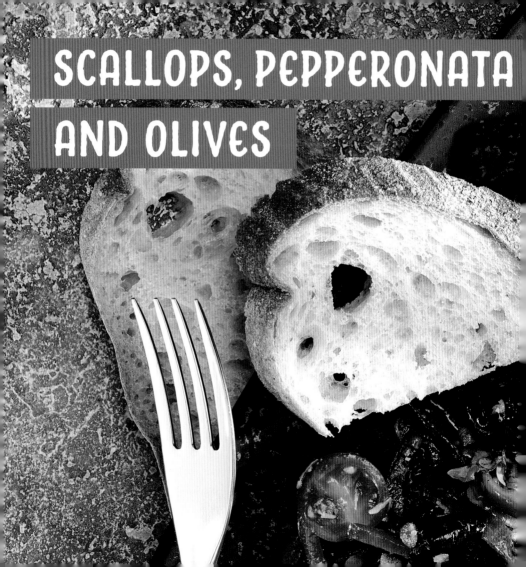

SCALLOPS, PEPPERONATA AND OLIVES

SCALLOPS, PEPPERONATA AND OLIVES

Ingredients:

12 large scallops

1 tbsp butter

½ lemon, juice only

6 red peppers, sliced

3 small red onions, sliced

½ head garlic, unpeeled

2 tbsp red wine vinegar

3 tbsp olive oil

1 tbsp capers

100g cherry tomatoes (sliced in half)

200g olives (sliced in half)

1 tbsp flat-leaf parsley, chopped

½ bunch basil, picked

Method:

- Add the sliced peppers and onions (½cm thick) to a roasting tray. Season with salt and pepper and a liberal amount of olive oil, then roast at 170°C for 10-15 minutes.

- At the same time, roast the garlic cloves in their skins in a separate tray for 10 minutes with a little oil.

- Once soft and cool enough to handle, remove the cloves from the skin and crush with the side of a knife.

- When the peppers and onions are cooked (softened but not mushy) and still warm, dress them with the remaining ingredients, mixing lightly to avoid destroying the textures of the roasted vegetables.

- Pan fry the scallops in a hot pan, finishing with butter and lemon, and serve with the pepperonata and crusty bread or rocket salad. This dish is best served warm rather than piping hot.

Not all scallops are created equal and to give specific cooking times is ultimately misleading, although a medium-large scallop will take two to three minutes on either side. When pan-frying scallops, they want to be as dry as possible, cooking with a small amount of oil and where necessary finished with butter. In a heavy-based frying pan with a high heat, sear the scallops on both sides to ensure a good colour.

STEAMED SCALLOPS WITH SOY, GINGER, HONEY AND SPRING ONIONS

STEAMED SCALLOPS WITH SOY, GINGER, HONEY AND SPRING ONIONS

Ingredients:

12-16 large prepared scallops, with the roe attached in the shell (ask your fishmonger)

2 tsp fresh ginger, grated

1 tbsp sesame oil

1 tbsp dark soy sauce

1 tbsp light soy sauce

½ tbsp rice vinegar

1 tsp honey

1 tbsp toasted sesame seeds

5 spring onions, sliced thin

Method:

- Mix the soy sauces, sesame oil, vinegar and honey in a small pan, heat gently until the honey dissolves and set aside.

- Add a small amount of ginger to each of the scallops.

- Using a wide, shallow pan with 3cm of water and a steamer on top, cook the scallops in the shells for around 4 minutes or until firm to the touch. If you only have a small steamer, put two scallops in each shell and follow the same steps to avoid having to cook multiple batches.

- Spoon the warm soy dressing over the scallops and top with the spring onions and toasted sesame seeds.

Scallops are one of the ultimate seafood treats. In the waters off the coast of North Wales, the fishing of scallops is rigorously regulated and the use of seabed-churning dredgers is given short shrift in favour of far more sustainable hand-diving.

MUSSELS

A nutritious, sustainable and delicious seafood choice, the versatility and health benefits of mussels make them a fantastic addition to your diet.

A celebrated North Wales foodstuff that grows naturally around our coastline, certain key areas, such as the Menai Strait, are especially perfect for the cultivation of sensational mussels.

- Mussels are highly nutritious, low in fat and an excellent source of lean protein, providing all the essential amino acids your body needs together with vitamins B12 and C, iron, selenium and omega-3 fatty acids.

- An environmentally friendly option, mussels are filter feeders, which means they help improve water quality by filtering and purifying the surrounding marine environment. Mussels are often farmed, making them a sustainable choice for seafood lovers.

- With a distinctive taste, often described as sweet and briny, mussels readily absorb the flavours they are cooked with, making them versatile and perfect for culinary experimentation.

- Mussels are relatively affordable compared to some other types of seafood and are widely available in seafood markets.

LOCAL, NATURAL
MUSSELS

Mussels have been harvested from beneath the waves of the River Conwy for hundreds of years. Despite the passing of time and the advanced technology that might now speed things up, Conwy mussels are still being fished the old-school way. If the month has an 'R' in it, as tradition demands, you'll find a small dory boat heading out to the Conwy mussel banks most mornings, rain or shine.

Trevor Jones, with over six decades of fishing experience ran the operation at Conwy Mussels for many years but these days the torch has been passed down to his son, Tom, who is understandably effusive when it comes to their daily catch: 'They're the best mussels in the world! They're different really on every level.'

He continues, 'They are natural mussels, which are quite hard to find now. So many of the mussels you buy are rope-grown or dredged, which is basically an artificial mussel bed. These are untouched; just nature taking its course, and they absolutely thrive.'

Tradition plays an important part in maintaining the standards. 'The mussel beds have been here for centuries, and we've always collected them and harvested them the same way with an old pitch-pine rake.

'It's a very small operation, there's only about three or four of us going out, plus my dad who's still doing it at his age, pushing 80 – not that you'd know to look at him. We've always been a niche market too which helps us to keep the quality high.'

But what about the taste? Many chefs, like Rick Stein and Phil Vickery, have been absolutely bowled over by the quality of

Now remember, scrub and clean the mussels first, especially if they are coated in barnacles and need debearding (i.e. pulling out the thin bits of seaweed. Lovely word, isn't it?).

Once they're cooked, those that haven't opened shouldn't be eaten.

Conwy's black diamonds, so what's the difference and why? According to Tom, 'We tend to have a plump, sweet-tasting, juicy mussel here, and we always say it's because they're in an estuary, so they're getting salt water from the sea and nutrients from fresh water coming down from the Welsh hills.'

Another key factor is that Conwy mussels are strictly seasonal. Come the end of April, the rakes are put back on the hooks and the mussel beds are given a good four months to recover and replenish. When September arrives, the sight of the boys heading out again on their boats is, for me, the first harbinger of autumn and a reminder that even though the weather's about to deteriorate, you know there's some damn fine eating ahead.

Mussels are an environmentally friendly way to feed yourself, particularly over the cold winter months. Efficient water purifiers themselves, North Wales mussels are responsibly sustained and packed full of nutrients – terribly good for warding off colds by all accounts!

I would heartily recommend that you pay Tom a visit in Conwy to see his operation in full flow. 'It's all done on the quay front,' says he. 'We have a protected food name because everything is done right here. They're treated and purified here on the quay. You can literally watch the process from the fishing to the plate! Watch us going out there with our rakes, watch us watering and treating them here, and if you give us seven quid you can take a bag home with you!'

www.conwymussels.com

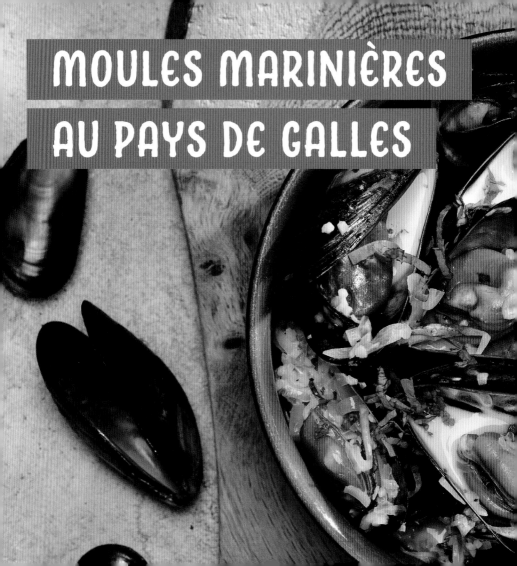

MOULES MARINIÈRES
AU PAYS DE GALLES

MOULES MARINIÈRES AU PAYS DE GALLES

Ingredients:

120g butter

2 shallots, finely sliced

1 leek, finely chopped

400ml white wine

2.5kg mussels

Small bunch flat-leaf parsley, finely chopped

100ml double cream

1 clove garlic, roughly chopped

Crusty bread

Method:

- Heat the butter in a large, heavy-bottomed pot on low heat. Once melted, add the garlic, leek and shallots and cook until soft.

- Throw in the white wine, a good pinch of salt and cracked pepper.

- Reduce by a third, then throw in the mussels and cover with a lid.

- After 7 minutes, shake the pot, then throw in the cream and flat-leaf parsley. Return the lid for a further 2 minutes.

- Serve straight away with crusty bread.

We tend to have a plump, sweet-tasting, juicy mussel here, and we always say it's because they're in an estuary, so they're getting salt water from the sea and nutrients from fresh water coming down from the Welsh hills.

STUFFED MUSSELS

STUFFED MUSSELS

Ingredients:

1kg mussels

2 shallots, finely chopped

1 sprig thyme

1 tbsp capers

20g pine nuts

100g butter

5 cloves garlic, chopped

½ bunch flat-leaf parsley

2 slices slightly stale white bread

50g Parmesan, grated

Method:

- Heat a heavy-bottomed pot. Once it's at a decent temperature (it doesn't need to be *red hot*), throw in your mussels and cover with a lid.

- Cook the mussels for 3-4 minutes or until they have all opened.

- While the mussels are cooking, place your bread and pine nuts into a food processor and give them a whizz to get them into a rough crumb consistency, then add all the remaining ingredients and a good pinch of salt and pepper.

- Take each mussel and carefully remove the meat. Place the mussel back into the larger part of the shell and top with about half a teaspoon of the stuffing mix.

- Preheat your grill and bake for 2-3 minutes until golden. Finish with a squeeze of lemon.

MACKEREL

Mackerel is a nutritional powerhouse, rich in omega-3 fatty acids and essential nutrients. Its versatility in cooking, health benefits and sustainability make it an excellent choice to incorporate into your diet.

- Mackerel has a distinct, rich and robust flavour able to pair well with a variety of ingredients. It can be prepared in various ways, from grilling and baking to smoking or even pickling.

- Mackerel is packed with high-quality protein and one of the richest sources of omega-3 fatty acids, particularly eicosapentaenoic acid (EPA) and docosahexaenoic acid (DHA). These essential fatty acids have been linked to various health benefits, including reducing inflammation, supporting heart health and promoting brain function.

- Many mackerel species have healthy populations and are responsibly harvested, meaning they are generally considered a sustainable seafood choice.

- Mackerel is accessible to a wide range of budgets and readily available in local shops and fish markets.

MACKEREL FISHING OFF THE MENAI STRAIT

In the early 1980s, my dad renovated an old Morecambe Bay Prawner, or Nobby, a beautiful wooden boat called 'Peggy'.

Every other weekend, we would head to Port Dinorwic (better known now as Y Felinheli*), near the Menai Strait, where 'Peggy' was moored. Off we'd sail, out into the North Sea, my dad every inch the bearded buccaneer at the rudder while mum prepped up some scran in the galley. My brother and I, mere kids, clipped to the guard-wires in our life-jackets and no use to man or beast, would trade *Jaws* quotes with each other and occasionally get sick.

Morecambe Bay Prawners were designed with an elliptical stern that was noticeably close to the water; close enough for my brother and I to dangle our little legs over the side and get our feet wet. On one such jaunt, we'd headed out to sea armed with our own mackerel lines, and with calm waters around us, we sat at the stern and dropped our lines over the side.

We must have lowered them directly into a vast shoal of fish because within minutes all of our lines were being yanked by something pulling away frenetically at the other end. With our memories of watching *Jaws* still quite vivid, we carefully lifted our legs out of the water for safety, then reeled in our catch – eight gleaming, iridescent Prussian-blue mackerel.

Quick as a flash, my mum gutted and filleted them, fried them up with butter and lemon juice and there under the sun we ate the world's freshest mackerel lunch off some Falcon enamelware plates, with hunks of granary bread to wipe everything up at the end. Even now, it remains one of the most delicious meals I have ever eaten – an instant awareness that some things can taste so good that they can alter your very view on life!

Mackerel still has something of a lower-tier reputation, possibly because what passes for 'mackerel', lying there on a bed of crushed ice in the supermarkets as withered as a leather purse, bears absolutely no resemblance whatsoever to the fresh stuff, which is wondrous, deeply flavoursome and unique – not to mention terribly, terribly good for you, teeming with all that omega 3 oil.

Here are some transformative mackerel recipes that really bring out the very best in this fantastic fish. Failing that: butter, lemon juice, granary bread and an old boat. You can't go wrong.

(*If you do go to Y Felinheli, head to the Garddfon Inn, the kind of pub you would *kill* to have as your local.)

'Prolific spawners, these sustainable and affordable fish are also high in omega 3. They are equally delicious served hot, cold, smoked or even cured.'
Toby Watson

MACKEREL RILLETTES, PICKLED BEETROOT AND CROSTINI

MACKEREL RILLETTES, PICKLED BEETROOT AND CROSTINI

Ingredients:

6 smoked mackerel fillets (skinless)

60g butter

½ bunch chives

½ tsp horseradish

50g soured cream

10g mayonnaise

1 shallot, finely chopped

1 clove garlic, crushed

¼ tsp paprika

3 uncooked beetroot

80ml white wine vinegar

100ml water

50ml sugar

1 tbsp mustard seeds

1 tbsp coriander seeds

1 crostini

Olive oil

Frisée salad

Method:

- In a saucepan, gradually warm the butter with the shallot and garlic, then flake in the mackerel and continue to break it up with a fork.

- Remove from the heat and stir in the herbs, soured cream, paprika and horseradish. Set aside to cool.

- For your crostini, thinly slice a ciabatta, brush with olive oil and a sprinkle of salt and bake in the oven on 100°C until crisp.

- Peel your beetroot and chop into wedges (about 8 per beet), place these in a saucepan with the water, vinegar, sugar, mustard and coriander seeds and simmer for 30 minutes until there is just enough liquid left to use as a dressing for your salad. Add more water if the liquid has disappeared before the beetroot is cooked.

- Leave to cool and serve alongside your mackerel and salad.

'One of my go to summer picnic classics. The smoked mackerel is edgy enough to stand up to the full-on fierceness of the pickled beetroot and horseradish. It also works really well if you freeze it and roll it in puff pastry to make a mackerel roll.'
Toby Watson

GRILLED MACKEREL, TOMATO, FETA AND CUCUMBER SALAD

GRILLED MACKEREL, TOMATO, FETA AND CUCUMBER SALAD

Ingredients:

4 mackerel fillets

200g cherry tomatoes, cut in half

1 whole cucumber, sliced

100g feta cheese

½ bunch basil, torn

2 garlic cloves, grated

1-2 tsp white wine vinegar

1-2 tsp caster sugar

1 lemon, cut into wedges

Method:

- Marinate the cut tomatoes with a pinch of salt, a pinch of sugar and a teaspoon of white wine vinegar. Mix gently and allow to sit for 30 minutes to bring the flavours out of the tomatoes.

- Meanwhile, slice the cucumber in half lengthwise and scoop out the seeds with a teaspoon, then cut into half moon slices, approximately ½cm thick.

- Add the cucumber slices and diced feta to the tomatoes (which by now will have released some juices) and mix very gently.

- Finish with torn basil leaves, a drizzle of good olive oil and season to taste with more salt, sugar and vinegar if needed (the salad should have a slight sweet and sour flavour).

- For the mackerel, rub the skin with oil and season with salt and pepper, then place under a hot grill for 3-4 minutes until the skin is crispy and the flesh is firm.

- Serve immediately on top of the salad with a wedge of lemon to squeeze over.

I highly recommend trying mackerel as a delicious and nutritious seafood option. Mackerel is known for its rich flavour and high levels of omega-3 fatty acids, which are beneficial for heart health. It's also a good source of protein, vitamins and minerals. Pairing mackerel with fresh herbs and lemon or a tangy sauce enhances its natural taste – give it a try, and you might discover a new favourite seafood dish!

COD

North Wales is blessed with abundant cod populations due to its proximity to the Irish Sea and North Atlantic Ocean. While most commonly associated with the quintessential fish and chips, it is a versatile ingredient which lends itself to a much wider variety of dishes.

- Cod has a mild and delicate flavour with broad appeal, ideal for use in various recipes and cuisines.

- Whether baked, grilled, pan-fried or used in stews and soups, the firm and flaky texture of cod makes it suitable for preparing to your preferences.

- Cod is widely available from local sources and relatively affordable when compared to some other varieties of seafood, making it an accessible option to try out.

- Cod is an excellent source of lean protein and low in calories and fat, making it a healthy choice for those watching their weight. Additionally, it contains essential vitamins and minerals such as vitamin B12, vitamin D and selenium. While not as rich in omega-3 fatty acids as some other fish, such as mackerel, it still contains a moderate amount of these healthy fats.

ENOCH'S FISH AND CHIPS

Cod was for many years a viciously maligned fish, completely unappreciated unless served in batter and doused in vinegar. How times have changed.

Fish have a habit of yo-yoing up and down within the seafood hierarchy. It wasn't that long ago that monkfish was being used as pub scampi or even cat food. Now it's an exorbitant treat, to be enjoyed only on special occasions that require sticking your hand deep into your pockets.

The issue of sustainability plays a large part in a fish's market value and that's a subject that's crucial to Danny White-Meir's business outlook. 'I read a book called *Cod* by Mark Kurlansky many years ago,' says Danny, 'and he talked about how cod was fished on the Grand Banks just off North America and how plentiful it was, and it was basically pillaged until there were literally none left. And if you can do that to millions of tonnes of fish, it really made me think, "Where's our fish coming from and how are we catching it?"

There's no such thing as an infinite supply of fish.'

Sustainability and ethics are front and centre factors in the success of Enoch's, his hugely popular fish and chip restaurant in Llandudno Junction, which came to my hungry family's rescue several times during lockdown when my children tired of my cooking! His family had been in the fish and chip business in Stoke-on-Trent since 1963, and when he arrived at Enoch's, the 15-year-old Danny was downstairs in the kitchen making fish cakes before he'd had time to unpack his bags.

'My stepfather was a second-generation fish fryer and his dad was very, very strict on the way of doing things: getting the batter right etc., and it stayed with him and with me too. Because of that, we were genuinely bothered about how it tasted, how it was made, how it was cooked, everything.'

'A brilliant cod hack which makes it look like you've put much more effort into it than you really have is to spread fresh pesto over the fish, then sprinkle Panko breadcrumbs over it before roasting in the oven. Very simple, very effective.' Cai Ross

Danny took over the business in 2006 and it was revamped to great acclaim, with sustainability at the forefront. 'We went to Tom Aiken's fish and chips restaurant off the King's Road in London and he was selling MSC cod loins, which were new to me. I got in touch with him and he told me all about MSC accredited fish, all the traceability factors that keep the quality high and maintain the sustainability. We've been supporters of this since we reopened and it's something that I think our customers really appreciate.'

With the gradual shrinking of the fishing industry in these parts, fresh cod became something of a rare but always welcome treat for us at Paysanne, when the fishermen used to pay us a visit. It's still caught fairly locally though, but not in great quantities. Whenever a fresh cod was presented, our old chef Bill, who was a passionate seafood devotee, would whoop with delight: 'Hahey! It's the good stuff!'

One of its great strengths is its versatility, as these recipes will demonstrate. Roast it, steam it, bake it, smoke it, cure it... Plus, of course, you can always head to a fish and chip shop and enjoy it as God intended – with a mug of tea and thick white bread.

www.enochs.co.uk

FISH AND CHIPS

FISH AND CHIPS

Ingredients:

1 litre vegetable oil

5 large potatoes, peeled and cut into 2-3cm chips

250g self-raising flour

3 tsp salt

250ml Welsh lager (Wild Horse is excellent but there's a plentiful selection available in North Wales)

4 x 170g pieces cod fillet or loin

Malt vinegar

Tartare sauce (see page 148)

Method:

- Warm the oil in a deep saucepan to about 155-165°C.

- Carefully place the chips in the pan and cook for 6 minutes before removing and placing them on some kitchen roll to drain off the excess fat.

- Place them in the fridge (this will draw out excess moisture and give them a proper crispy crust).

- Create a well in the middle of the flour and add 1 tsp of salt, then slowly start incorporating the beer into the flour, whisking to avoid lumps.

- Dust the fish in plain flour and increase the oil temperature to about 170°C.

- Lower the fish into the batter and cook for 7-8 minutes until golden.

- Remove and place them in the oven at about 150°C to keep warm while the chips have their final cook.

- Drop the chips back into the fryer and finish them off (they should take a further 3 or 4 minutes – you'll know by trying one!).

- Serve with plenty of salt and vinegar and tartare sauce.

PAN-FRIED COD WITH BLACK PUDDING AND CANNELLINI BEANS

PAN-FRIED COD WITH BLACK PUDDING AND CANNELLINI BEANS

Ingredients:

4 x 200g pieces skinned cod loin

250g cannellini beans, soaked overnight

50ml olive oil

1 onion, finely chopped

1 carrot, finely chopped

4 cloves

1 tsp smoked paprika

2 chorizo sausages, thickly sliced

4 rashers streaky smoked bacon

100g black pudding, diced

50g tomato purée

200g belly pork

½ bunch flat-leaf parsley, chopped

Method:

- Place the belly pork and beans in a large pan and bring to the boil. Simmer for 30 minutes.

- Drain and discard the liquid. Return the pan to the heat and add the olive oil.

- Chop up the belly pork and throw it in along with the chorizo, smoked bacon, carrot, onion and garlic. Cook this for a further 8 minutes until the chorizo juices start to be released.

- Add the beans, paprika, tomato purée and cover with water, cooking until the beans are soft (you'll need to keep adding water in small amounts).

- 10 minutes before the beans are cooked, add the black pudding and reduce the mix to stew-like consistency. Season with salt and pepper.

- Remove from the heat and stir through the flat leaf parsley.

- Place the cod loin on a baking tray and brush with olive oil, salt and pepper. Bake for 8-10 minutes at 180°C.

- To serve, spoon the bean mix into four warm bowls and place one baked cod loin on top of each.

'There is something about pork and beans. They were made for each other. This is a step up from the tinned variety, with the addition of black pudding, bacon, belly pork and chorizo propelling it into a winter warmer that's fit for a banquet.'
Toby Watson

PEPPERED COD, WILD MUSHROOMS AND BÉARNAISE SAUCE

PEPPERED COD, WILD MUSHROOMS AND BÉARNAISE SAUCE

Ingredients:

4 x 200g skinned cod fillets

40g cracked black pepper

60g flour

Olive oil

500g wild mushrooms, chopped

1 bunch flat-leaf parsley, chopped

50g butter

4 cloves garlic, finely chopped

2 shallots, finely chopped

25ml brandy

1 bag baby spinach

200ml Béarnaise sauce (see page 150)

Method:

- Preheat the oven to 200°C.

- Dry off the cod fillets and dust them in the flour and cracked black pepper.

- Heat the olive oil in a frying pan and cook the fish fillets skin-side down for 3 minutes on each side.

- Transfer the fillets to a baking tray and cook in the oven for a further 5-7 minutes.

- Meanwhile, melt the butter in the pan with the garlic and shallots and cook for 4 minutes, then add the mushrooms and cook through on a high heat for 5 minutes.

- Just before they are ready, add the brandy and reduce, then throw in the spinach, count to 20 and turn the pan heat off (the spinach will wilt down with the residual heat in the pan).

- Season with plenty of salt and black pepper.

'People are too shy when it comes to peppering.
If I have a fiery peppered steak then I want a punch-packing hit to the culinary senses, not a mild waft. Similarly, béarnaise needs the acidity of a good reduction and plenty of tarragon. Be bold.'
Toby Watson

BRANDADE

Ingredients:

200g cod fillet, chopped into 10 pieces

140g sea salt

140g sugar

160g double cream

6 cloves garlic, crushed

100ml extra virgin olive oil

¼ bunch flat-leaf parsley, chopped

45g breadcrumbs

Pinch rosemary and thyme, chopped

Method:

- Wash and dry the fillet of cod. Place half of the sugar and salt mix in a dish and lay the cod on top, cover with the remaining salt and sugar mix and pat it on, covering completely. Refrigerate for 48 hours.

- Once the cod has firmed up, rinse off the salt and pat dry.

- Place the salt cod in a bowl of cold water and soak for 24 hours to let it rehydrate.

- In a large pot, bring the cream, garlic, rosemary and thyme to the boil, then add the fish and leave to simmer until soft.

- Remove the fish and reduce the liquor by about a half. Flake the fish back into the cream mix and slowly incorporate the olive oil, then add the flat leaf parsley.

- Spoon the mix into a dish, top with breadcrumbs and bake on 180°C until the top is golden.

SALT AND PEPPER COD, RICE NOODLE SALAD

Ingredients:

100g vermicelli rice noodles

600g cod loin, chopped into about 20 equally sized pieces

50g salt and pepper mix

1 litre vegetable oil

3 tbsp cornflour

1 red chilli

½ cucumber, thinly sliced

3 spring onions, thinly sliced

1 bunch coriander, chopped

4 lime wedges

2 tbsp sesame oil

50ml Thai dressing

Method:

- Mix the cornflour and salt and pepper mix together in a bowl. Add the fish and give it a toss to make sure it's all covered. Leave to sit for 10 minutes.

- Bring a 1 litre pan of water to the boil and throw in your rice noodles. Turn off the heat and leave to stand for 7 minutes.

- Drain under cold water and immediately add the sesame oil to stop them clumping together. Throw in your salad ingredients and mix through.

- Just before serving add your Thai dressing and mix through.

- Heat 1 litre of vegetable oil to 170°C in a high-sided saucepan and drop in your fish nuggets. Cook for 5-6 minutes until crispy and golden. Serve with lime wedge and salad.

TROUT

With a distinct flavour profile, trout is another versatile seafood experience to enjoy. In North Wales there are many sites where you can fish for trout yourself, both at local fisheries or wild fishing along our rivers.

- The firm flesh of trout holds up well to various types of preparation, allowing for culinary creativity and experimentation. It can be grilled, baked, pan-fried or even smoked to enhance its flavour.

- A nutrient-dense fish, trout provides a range of essential vitamins and minerals, including omega-3 fatty acids, vitamins B12, D and selenium.

- Trout is widely available fresh or frozen in local shops and fish markets and often caught by recreational anglers.

- Trout is often farmed, making it a more sustainable seafood option. Responsible fishing and fish farming practices help to reduce the environmental impact associated with wild fish populations.

CEFNI ANGLING ASSOCIATION

The coastline of North Wales is hugely popular with sea-anglers, but Gwynedd, Conwy, Denbighshire and Flintshire are linked by arteries of rivers, all boasting a different kind of catch. Peppered along the banks of the River Conwy and the Dee, the Glaslyn, Mawddach, Elwy or the River Clwyd, you'll often spot someone sat meditatively on a stool, keeping an eye on their fishing line, while sipping from a Thermos and possibly listening to the cricket on the radio, all the time hoping that a curious carp, tench, chub or rainbow trout will eventually take the bait.

There are also several fishing lakes in North Wales, where professional anglers swap tips with up-and-comers, all of them hoping their patience pays off with a photograph of themselves holding a gargantuan fish. One of the very best of these lakes is Llyn Cefni in the heart of Anglesey. Charles Meadows, the honorary secretary of the Angling Association there, is a passionate advocate for the sport and caught the fishing bug many years ago.

'Like most young boys living in the country in the 1960s, my dad took me with him whilst literally fishing for our supper – we would eat whatever we (he) caught, especially if he managed to catch an eel or a pike, and this was my introduction to fishing. It served one purpose, and that was to put food on the table.'

School and life in general relegated Charles's childhood fishing adventures to the past, but in the late '70s a friend introduced him to a river bailiff who taught him the art of fly fishing for trout. 'This was a revelation for me. I took to it instantly. No more standing or sitting on the bank drowning a worm or a maggot, but a whole new horizon and ambition.

'There were many skills to learn and practice: how to read the water and gauge conditions where a wily trout might be lurking ready to pounce on an artificial fly, entomology and the art of fly tying so as to copy the natural insect life and, of course, the art of casting a fly.

'Fishing suddenly became an active, challenging, interesting and above all enjoyable hobby. Many hours spent in the open air in all weathers in beautiful surroundings and with the occasional good banter back in the hut, and all this in the idyllic surroundings of Anglesey. What more could a hobby provide?'

Trout are fairly readily available to buy all around the country. More often than not, they tend to be farmed and are pleasant enough. Fresh rainbow trout, though, caught in a clean river, are a regal treat: light, pink and delicate. Come the season – which is strictly regulated – sea trout (or *sewin*, as they are known in Wales) arrive and are to the fish world what Elvis Presley was to rock 'n' roll.

Essentially a combination of the finest salmon and the greatest trout, simply cooked *sewin* is an annual treat that has been a high-point of the summer for many years. If you can hunt it down, you might find smoked coracle-caught *sewin*, which is an opulent alternative to smoked salmon.

For the ultimate experience, though, you'll need to pull on your waders and catch one yourself. Just ask Charles Meadows: 'To catch a hard-fighting trout on a fly that you have tied yourself, to land it and proudly take it home to cook and enjoy is an absolute pleasure.' Charles's favourite cooking method is to hot-smoke the fillets in a small home smoker and serve with a simple salad and new potatoes. 'Alternatively, and even tastier, is the smoked trout pâté my wife conjures up.'

Here are a few other ideas to get the best out of your hard-earned catch.

www.llyncefni.co.uk

SMOKED TROUT AND PEA FUSILLI, WITH PECORINO CHEESE

Ingredients:

300g fusilli pasta

150g peas

2 smoked trout fillets

1 bunch chives, finely chopped

1 tsp horseradish

50ml extra virgin olive oil

2 lemons, juice only

Pecorino cheese

Method:

- Cook the pasta in boiling salted water to *al dente*.

- For the last 5 minutes, add the peas.

- Drain the pasta and throw in the flaked smoked trout, olive oil, horseradish and half of the chives.

- Return to the heat to warm the fish through.

- Season with lemon juice and top with the remaining chives and finely grated Pecorino cheese.

'We normally have some sort of smoked fish in the fridge at home and there's always a hard cheese and peas in the freezer. This is one of those meals that you can knock up in five minutes, whilst the kids are nagging, "Is dinner ready yet?"'
Toby Watson

CURED SEA TROUT, PICKLED VEGETABLES AND WASABI MAYONNAISE

Ingredients for curing:

600g skinless sea trout

50g sea salt

30g sugar

1 bunch dill

Method:

- Mix the dry ingredients together and pack around the sea trout. Clingfilm tightly and leave for 72 hours.

- Remove and wash off the curing liquor, then slice thinly.

- To serve, arrange the fish on a plate and neatly scatter the pickles and some dots of the wasabi mayonnaise.

- Feel free to add a leaf; micro rocket works well, or just some shoots of watercress.

Ingredients for pickling:

50ml cider vinegar

40ml white wine

50ml water

10g sugar

25g mustard seeds

1 cucumber (outer layer only), finely diced

1 halved red onion, thinly sliced

Method:

- Bring the vinegar, wine, water, sugar and mustard seeds to the boil and set aside for 24 hours. Marinate the cucumber and red onion separately in the pickling liquor (just enough to cover them).

Ingredients for wasabi mayonnaise:

1 egg yolk

1 tsp white wine vinegar

½ tsp wasabi paste

120ml olive oil

1 lemon, juice only

Method:

- In a blender, whisk up the egg yolk with the vinegar and wasabi paste, then slowly add the oil, whisking continuously until it emulsifies, or thickens. Season with salt, pepper and the lemon juice.

OYSTERS

Oysters hold a special place in the culinary scene of North Wales, sourced from the region's pristine coastal waters that help develop a rich, briny taste with hints of sweetness.

- Oysters are packed with essential nutrients like zinc, iron, vitamin B12 and omega-3 fatty acids and are an excellent source of protein and low in fat.

- Considered an environmentally friendly seafood option, as filter feeders oysters can help improve water quality by filtering and purifying the surrounding marine environment.

- Oysters can be enjoyed in various ways, including raw, served in half the shell, baked, grilled, or incorporated into other seafood dishes and sauces. Accompanying them with sauces is a popular way to explore different flavour combinations.

MENAI OYSTERS

Oysters have something of a Marmite reputation – I don't think I've ever met anyone with an indifferent opinion about them. They either start salivating there and then or pull the kind of face a fussy child might deploy when confronted with a broccoli and asparagus salad. I was hesitant at first and it took a few cowardly dress-rehearsal arm-swings until I finally managed to tip one down my gullet. It was in Rules in Covent Garden, washed down with a glass of chilled Muscadet, and it was love at first bite: a creamy, saline smack that hits you like a wave breaking across the back of your mouth. Ironically, the oysters we were devouring – we ordered another plate in the end – were grown less than half an hour from Paysanne, on the Anglesey coast.

The Menai Oysters and Mussels Co. was set up in 1994 by marine biologist Shaun Krijnen. Set amongst some of the most wondrous sea views in North Wales in a Special Area of Conservation, the oysters grown here have been wowing seafood aficionados for over two decades. But what's the secret...?

'In a nutshell,' says Shaun, 'it's the water. There's the combination of managing the stock and getting the husbandry right too, but the fact is that nature is doing the lion's share of the work. There's very little input from me.'

Trained as a marine biologist, Shaun's devotion to his oyster beds springs from a passion for ecological preservation. 'Oysters are a vitally important keystone species. There is nothing as environmentally sound as farming shellfish. They are grown in a way comparable to the way they would grow in the wild anyway. The natural way that the sea tends to impart nitrogen and phosphorus and all the planktonic food that oysters need to thrive is an entirely organic process.'

More and more people in the UK are getting over their oyster unease and enjoying them in greater numbers than ever. Even if you baulk at the idea of raw oysters, they are impressively versatile –

'I didn't like oysters until my late teens, then I went to a grand old place in Guernsey and was served oysters Rockefeller. It was a dish that I remember to this day.'
Toby Watson

they work famously well in steak pies, for example. Shaun has even joined forces with local Llanfairpwll Distillery to make an Oyster Gin!

This means that Menai Oysters are thriving, but Shaun does sound a note of caution. 'Climate change is certainly making an impact, particularly with the rising sea temperatures. When I started twenty-seven years ago, year three to four is when you would normally see the vast majority of the oysters ready to harvest, now it's between years two to three, so a whole year has been shaved off.'

So a silver lining to the climate change cloud? More oysters? 'Not really.

Eventually, the sea will become more acidic, and being a bivalve based on calcium carbonate they will have to work harder for them to make their shell, which could change everything.'

www.menaioysters.co.uk

HOW TO OPEN AN OYSTER WITHOUT LOSING A LIMB

- First thing's first: don't cut corners and try to do this with a spoon handle or some cheap blunt cutlery. Get hold of a proper oyster knife (or shucker) with a bulb handle. That's your first stop to bypassing a trip to A&E!

- Hold the oyster flat side up with a thick tea-towel, making sure the hinge of the oyster is sticking out.

- Carefully slide the oyster knife under the hinge. It might take a few goes, but it will slide in eventually.

- Once you're in, carefully guide the knife around the lip of the oyster until you get all the way around, keeping the oyster level at all times. Turn the oyster knife a little to lift the lid, then you'll be able to lift it up fully with your fingers. Keeping it level means that you won't lose any of the liquid.

- When you've lifted the lid off completely, slide the blade carefully underneath the oyster and cut it away from the shell, slicing through the muscle that holds it there.

- Gently place your handiwork down onto a plate and get cracking with the rest of the oysters. Don't forget the tea towel!

- For some, there is no better way to eat oysters than to tip them down your gullet there and then (perhaps with a dash of Tabasco sauce and lemon juice). If you fancy something a little more creative to offer your guests, read on...

OYSTERS ROCKEFELLER

OYSTERS ROCKEFELLER

Ingredients:

24 oysters

250g unsalted butter

1 celery stalk, finely chopped

½ fennel bulb, finely chopped

3 shallots, finely chopped

1 clove garlic, crushed

1 bunch flat-leaf parsley, roughly chopped

1 bunch watercress

2 tbsp Pastis

2 tbsp Frank's hot sauce (or equally hot alternative)

70g breadcrumbs

2 lemons

Method:

- Open the top of the oysters and remove the oyster meat.

- Return the oyster to the bottom half of the shell, retaining as much of the liquid as possible.

- In a large pan, melt the butter and add the celery, fennel, shallots, garlic, parsley, watercress and a large pinch of salt.

- Cook for 3-4 minutes, then blend the mixture. Add the hot sauce, breadcrumbs and Pastis and purée.

- Spoon two teaspoons of the mix onto the oysters and grill for 10-12 minutes until golden and bubbling.

- Squeeze over the lemons and serve.

SEA BASS

North Wales sea bass combines exquisite flavour, sustainable fishing practices, nutritional benefits and culinary versatility.

- The clean, cold waters of the North Wales region contribute to the exceptional flavour of locally caught sea bass.

- The area's responsible fishing practices emphasise long-term sustainability.

- A nutritious fish and a good source of lean protein, sea bass is packed with essential omega-3 fatty acids, as well as vitamins and minerals.

- Whether pan-seared, grilled, baked or served raw as sashimi, sea bass is adaptable to different cooking methods and desired flavours.

HARVESTING SEA SALT

One of North Wales's biggest international success stories is Halen Môn sea salt. It is the brainchild of Alison and David Lea-Wilson, who started the business over 20 years ago, having already set up the popular Anglesey Sea Zoo in Brynsiencyn. The idea of harvesting salt from the waters off the Anglesey coast was sparked by a fortuitous incident involving a pan of sea water, an Aga stove and a moment of forgetfulness. It was clear after just one taste that the salt they were left with in the pan was no ordinary condiment.

'As part of our application to the EU for Protected Status we had to show that the raw material we used (seawater) was different to other seas and the way we made the salt gave a finished product with specific and special characteristics,' Alison told me. 'The lack of heavy industries and shipping, coupled with the strong twice-daily tides means that the water is fresh and clean. The minerals differ slightly seasonally as in the summer the shellfish – oysters and mussels – take a lot of the calcium out of the water. This means we have to rinse it less – great for our salt harvesters!'

Having grown up in Hampshire, Alison travelled to North Wales to study at Bangor University, where she fell for David and also the surrounding area. 'We both came up to university here and fell in love with the countryside and beaches. We found people were very friendly and accepting and tolerant of our attempts to start and run different businesses.'

Since it started in 1997, Halen Môn (*trans.* Anglesey Salt) has gone from being a well-kept local secret to being a much-prized addition to restaurants and kitchens in 22 countries around the world. Guests at royal weddings, Olympic ceremonies and political summits have all enjoyed this dynamic taste of pure, raw North Wales and Barack Obama no less is said to be an avid sprinkler of Halen Môn.

'A staple of European menus, in Italy it's *branzino*, in Spain it's *lubina*, but my favourite is the French translation, *loup de mer*, "wolf of the sea"'.
Toby Watson

These days, you can buy their salt intensified with flavours as diverse as garlic, umami and charcoal. What of Alison's choice of fish to go with it though? 'I recently cooked a brined lemon sole which was absolutely sublime. The brining firmed the flesh, making it almost impossible to overcook, and I served it with brown butter and rhubarb. And of course, whole turbot or sea bass baked in a salt crust is always a crowd pleaser.'

Ah yes, sea bass. Sea bass appear to enjoy the North Wales coast and we in turn enjoy having them here. A sublime, delicately flavoured fish, sea bass are, like bream, farmed successfully around the world and enjoy widespread popularity. The farmed version is pretty acceptable, but nothing to make a song and dance out of. Wild sea bass on the other hand is truly such stuff as dreams are made on.

During the summer months, the dusky shadows falling across the beaches of North Wales often feature the silhouettes of shore fishermen stretching their long lines out to sea. Chances are it's a wild sea bass that they're after, and who could possibly blame them?

Like mullet or sea bream, sea bass are the ideal fish for cooking whole on a barbecue. Here are a selection of recipes to enhance one of the finest ingredients you can catch on the end of a fishing line.

Let's start with Alison Lea-Wilson's choice: baked in a salt crust. I wonder what salt she uses...

www.halenmon.com

SEA BASS IN A SALT CRUST, WITH LEMON AND CAPER DRESSING

Ingredients:

1 whole wild sea bass (approx 750g)

600g sea salt (ideally Halen Môn!)

5 egg whites

Handful fresh dill

1 tsp Herbes de Provence

1 lemon, thinly sliced

Method:

- Preheat the oven to 180°C.

- To make the crust, whisk up to 5 egg whites to soft peaks. Chop the dill and fold into the egg mixture along with the Herbes de Provences. Mix all of the salt into this – it will form a kind of paste. If it's too dry, add a splash of water.

- Remove the head and tail from the sea bass and trim off the fins. Open the cavity of the fish and stuff with thin slices of lemon.

- On a baking sheet, lay approximately one third of the mixture in a line along the centre in the shape of a fish.

- Place the fish on top, then cover with the remaining mixture, making sure the fish is covered on all sides, then place it in the oven for 25-30 minutes. The mixture will look crispy.

- Take to the table and crack open, to the sound of gasps and applause from your dinner guests. Serve with a lemon and caper dressing.

A sublime, delicately flavoured fish, sea bass are, like bream, farmed successfully around the world and enjoy widespread popularity. The farmed version is pretty acceptable, but nothing to make a song and dance out of. Wild sea bass, on the other hand, is truly such stuff as dreams are made on.

SEA BASS CEVICHE WITH AVOCADO

SEA BASS CEVICHE WITH AVOCADO

Ingredients:

300g ultra fresh bass (skinless)

2 shallots, finely chopped

1 tbsp coriander leaves, chopped

1 green chilli, deseeded and diced

4 tbsp lime juice

2 mint leaves, finely chopped

1 plum tomato, deseeded and finely chopped

75ml extra virgin olive oil

½ avocado

30ml soured cream

Pinch cayenne pepper

1 clove garlic, crushed

Method:

- You can marinate ceviche for minutes or hours depending on your preference. The longer it marinates the more it firms up texturally.

- To make the marinade, mix the shallots, green chilli and 3 tablespoons of lime juice with the olive oil.

- Thinly slice your bass (1cm thick) and cover with the marinade (I leave it in the fridge for about an hour).

- Just before serving, fold the coriander and mint leaves through, along the finely chopped tomato.

- To make the avocado, simply blitz up 1 tbsp lime juice, half an avocado, 30ml of soured cream, the cayenne pepper and the garlic. Season with salt and pepper and dot on top of your fish.

'I like to cure mine for about an hour to get the texture that I'm looking for. The basic rule is that the longer you cure it, the more it will firm up.'
Toby Watson

BAKED SEA BASS WITH KALAMATA OLIVES, CAPERS AND LEMONS

Ingredients:

4 sea bass fillets, skin on

2 tbsp oregano, chopped

2 tbsp pine nuts, crushed

1 lemon, thinly sliced

1 lemon, juice only

1 tbsp capers, chopped

2 red peppers, roasted and sliced

½ thyme bunch, chopped

2 red onions, sliced

16 kalamata olives, pitted

8 cloves garlic

50ml olive oil

Method:

- Firstly, warm the olive oil and garlic cloves in a small pan for 10 minutes over a low heat to soften the garlic.

- Slash the skin on the sea bass at 2 cm intervals and season with salt and black pepper.

- Place on a baking tray, sat on top of the sliced lemons, olives, red onions and roasted peppers, along with the garlic and thyme, and bake at 200°C for 10-12 minutes.

- Meanwhile, make your pine nut dressing by mixing together the oregano, pine nuts, capers and olive oil with a generous pinch of salt.

- Once the fish is out of the oven, give it a good dressing and serve.

SEA BASS WITH GINGER, CHILLI AND SPRING ONIONS

Ingredients:

4 sea bass fillets

50ml rapeseed oil

1 tbsp sesame oil

50g ginger, thinly sliced into matchsticks

5 cloves garlic, thinly sliced

1 bunch spring onions, thinly sliced

2 red chillies, deseeded and thinly sliced

30ml soy sauce

Method:

- Slash the skin of the bass at 2cm intervals and season with salt.

- Heat half the rapeseed oil in a pan and lower in your fish. Cook for 5-6 minutes – you'll notice the sides starting to turn opaque.

- Turn the fish over and cook for a further 2 minutes (the skin should be nice and crispy).

- Remove from the pan and pop them in the oven to keep them warm, then turn the pan up to full and add the rest of the oils.

- Throw in the garlic, ginger and chillies and cook for 1 minute, then add your spring onions, give it a toss around, and splash in your soy sauce.

- Serve immediately on top of the fish.

BARBECUED SEA BASS
TACOS 'AL PASTOR'

BARBECUED SEA BASS TACOS 'AL PASTOR'

Ingredients:

3 sea bass fillets, skins slashed

4 cloves garlic, peeled

2 tsp salt

2 tbsp achiote paste

1 tbsp Mexican oregano

10ml olive oil

1 small onion

20ml cider vinegar

Ingredients for the salsa and slaw:

200g pineapple, diced

2 limes, juice only

2 whole green chillies

6 cherry tomatoes

3 cloves garlic, crushed

½ bunch coriander, chopped

¼ red cabbage, thinly sliced

2 lemons, juice only

1 tsp salt

Method:

- Firstly, make the marinade by combining the garlic, salt, achiote, oregano, olive oil, onion and vinegar with a hand blender. Rub these all over the fish and leave to marinate for 2-3 hours. Finish by cooking over smoking coals skin-side down. When it's time to fill the tacos, flake the bass into large chunks and get filling.

Method:

- Throw the chillies, garlic and tomatoes into a dry pan and char for 10 minutes. Empty the contents of the pan onto a chopping board and run a knife through it until finely chopped. In the meantime, return the pan to the heat with the pineapple and char well. Mix the pineapple in with the chilli and tomato mix and stir in the coriander and lime juice. For the slaw, pour the lemon juice over the cabbage and salt and crush by hand for 5 minutes (leave for 1 hour to allow the cabbage to soften).

Ingredients for tacos:

100g masa flour

¼ tsp salt

60ml hot water

1 tbsp olive oil

Method:

- Mix all the ingredients together in a bowl until a smooth dough forms. If it's too wet, add more flour; if it's too dry, add more water. Roll the mix into 12 equal-sized balls. Chill, then roll them out with a rolling pin or press them if you have a taco press. (Really, you have a taco press? Get you!) Cook them in a dry pan for 1 minute on each side. Cover them in a tea towel to keep them warm while you're cooking the others.

'I spent a lot of time in lockdown learning about the intricacies of Mexican food. One of the things I love about these is the theatre of plonking them on the table and people digging in, although in our house it also becomes quite a competitive experience!'
Toby Watson

SEA BASS WITH

ASPARAGUS AND

SAUCE VIERGE

SEA BASS WITH ASPARAGUS AND *SAUCE VIERGE*

Ingredients:

20ml olive oil

80g butter

4 sea bass fillets

12 asparagus spears,
ends trimmed off

3 plum tomatoes

30g capers

1 lemon, juice only

2 shallots, finely chopped

100ml extra virgin olive oil

½ bunch basil, chopped

½ bunch chives, chopped

¼ bunch flat-leaf parsley, chopped

Method:

- To make the sauce, plunge the tomatoes into boiling water for 3 minutes until the skin starts to come away.

- Refresh in cold water, discard the seeds and chop and retain the outer flesh.

- In a saucepan, add the extra virgin olive oil, shallots, tomatoes, garlic and capers and warm through (do not boil).

- After 5 minutes, remove from the heat and stir in the herbs and lemon juice, season with a little salt and leave to stand for 20 minutes. The sauce can be served cold, but if you want it warm just return it to the heat for 30 seconds before serving.

- Slash the skin of the sea bass at 3cm intervals and season with plenty of salt.

- Heat the olive oil in a frying pan and lower in the sea bass, skin-side down. Cook for 5 minutes until the sides start to go slightly opaque, then flip it over, throw in the butter and asparagus and cook for a further 3 minutes.

- Serve over the beautiful *sauce vierge*.

PLAICE

Plaice might well be the most prolific fish caught off the North Wales coast, yet has something of a muted reputation. No longer limited to being deep-fried to within an inch of its life, a good-sized, thick, fresh plaice is a delicate, fragile and flavoursome fish that melts in the mouth.

- Plaice has a delicate and mild flavour that has broad appeal, described as sweet, delicate and slightly nutty.

- A good source of lean protein, plaice is also rich in vitamins such as vitamin B12 and minerals like selenium, phosphorus and magnesium.

- Plaice can be prepared in a variety of ways, with its firm texture making it delicious whether grilled, pan-fried, baked or even used in dishes like fish tacos or seafood stir-fries.

- With well-managed populations and responsible fishing practices, choosing plaice supports sustainable fishing and helps maintain healthy marine ecosystems.

- Simultaneously light and filling, plaice is a fantastic summer fish that – unlike Dover sole – won't break the bank.

FRIED PLAICE BRUSCHETTA WITH CAESAR MAYONNAISE

FRIED PLAICE BRUSCHETTA WITH CAESAR MAYONNAISE

Ingredients:

4 plaice fillets

Vegetable oil, for frying

1 egg, beaten with 50ml milk

200g breadcrumbs and ¼ tsp salt

4 thick ciabatta slices

12 marinated anchovies

100g pancetta, diced

Method:

- Throw the pancetta into a frying pan with a tiny splash of oil and fry for 5 minutes until crispy.

- Remove the pancetta, then char the ciabatta in the same pan with the pancetta oils.

- Dip the plaice fillets in the breadcrumbs, then in the egg and finally the breadcrumbs again.

- Heat a non-stick pan and fry the plaice in 1-2cm of vegetable oil for 3 or 4 minutes on each side until golden.

- Spread the Caesar mayonnaise on the bruschetta and arrange with 1 or 2 leaves of the gem lettuce, a piece of the fried plaice along with the pancetta, marinated anchovies and parmesan shavings. Drizzle a bit more of the Caesar mayo on top to finish.

Ingredients for the mayonnaise:

1 clove garlic, crushed

4 marinated anchovies, finely chopped

50g Parmesan, grated

¼ tsp mustard

150g mayonnaise

1 lemon, juice only

Method:

- Mix all the ingredients together and season with salt and black pepper.

'A lot of people think that the Caesar salad is an Italian dish, however, it was created in Mexico during prohibition and brought back to these shores by the aristocracy of the day.'
Toby Watson

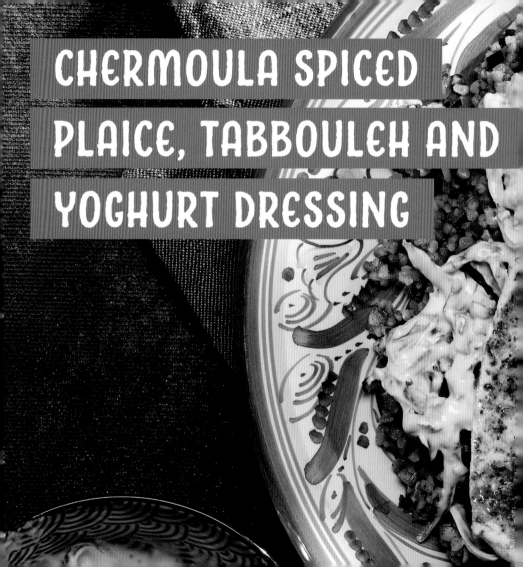

CHERMOULA SPICED PLAICE, TABBOULEH AND YOGHURT DRESSING

CHERMOULA SPICED PLAICE, TABBOULEH AND YOGHURT DRESSING

Ingredients for the fish and marinade:

1 bunch coriander

1 bunch flat-leaf parsley

1 tsp paprika

1 tsp cumin powder

1 tsp curry powder

1 tsp salt

Olive oil

1 lime, juice and zest

1 lemon, juice and zest

4 plaice fillets

Method:

- In a food processor, whizz up the herbs, spices, salt and lime and lemons. Use just enough olive oil to create a paste.

- Cover the fish with the paste.

- In a warm frying pan, heat 50ml of olive oil and fry the fish for 3-4 minutes on both sides.

Ingredients for tabbouleh:

1 bunch coriander, chopped

1 bunch mint, chopped

1 bunch flat-leaf parsley, chopped

1 red onion, finely chopped

1 clove garlic, crushed

2 lemons, juice only

1 tsp curry powder

80g bulgar wheat

Method:

- Soak the bulgar wheat in boiling water for 7-8 minutes, then rinse under cold water to remove the starch.

- Once drained, add the remaining ingredients and season with salt and pepper.

Ingredients for yoghurt dressing:

½ cucumber

½ bunch mint, chopped

1 tsp white wine vinegar

½ tsp sugar

2 cloves garlic, crushed

¼ tsp salt

250g Greek yoghurt

Method:

- Coarsely grate the outer layers of the cucumber, leave for 20 minutes and discard any excess liquid.

- Add the cucumber to the remaining ingredients and serve.

CRAB AND LOBSTER

Whether appreciated in classic dishes or explored through new recipes, North Wales crab and lobster are known for their exceptional freshness and high quality, with the short distance between the catch and your plate ensuring the most flavourful possible produce.

- Crab and lobster meat has a sweet, delicate and distinctive flavour that can vary depending on the species and preparation, offering a range of flavours to explore.

- From crab cakes to salads and soups, or simply steamed and served with butter or a flavourful sauce, the tender and succulent meat lends itself well to different cooking methods.

- Eating crab and lobster is often a social event experience. It is commonly associated with gatherings, such as crab feasts or seafood boils, where friends and family come together to crack shells and savour the succulent meat.

- Many species of crab and lobster are sustainably harvested, with regulations in place to protect their populations and the marine environment meaning buying sustainably sourced crab supports responsible fishing practices.

CRAB AND LOBSTER FISHING OFF THE NORTH WALES COAST

When I chatted to veteran fisherman and local legend Carl Davies, I had a crash-course in the secrets of fishing for crabs and lobsters.

'You see those big green masses out to sea? That's algae,' Carl explains. 'Nothing likes the algae. Once it disappears, the lobsters start to flourish. Not just the lobsters but everything. Mackerel, bass, they all start coming in. The algae uses up all the nutrients. The nutrients have built up all through the winter in the water because it's constantly been mixed up by storms and the nutrients come off the bottom into the water column. When the days lengthen and the temperature gets to a certain level in the spring, the algae starts blooming, and then it's not limited by anything until the nutrients, nitrates and phosphates are all used up. After that, it just dies. You see it in big, gloopy masses. Then it becomes food for all the lobster larvae and the crab larvae, and the fish time their spawning to coincide with this. So no one really likes it because the fishing isn't very good, but you just have to bear with it because it's what makes the world go round.'

If you take a stroll down Conwy quay, you'll see stacks upon stacks of Carl's lobster pots. They look like set dressing from an episode of *Poldark*, but then lobster fishing is a long-standing tradition and the methods have never really changed. You need a lobster pot, some bait, well-sharpened knowledge of local lobster habits and a lot of patience.

Carl's skills as a crab and lobster fisherman were honed from a very early age. 'Dad was a fisherman on the *Lady Gwen* and the business has been going since 1964. He used to be the coxswain at Llandudno lifeboats for about 35 years, so I was out with him from the age of six, mainly angling, pretty much every weekend. Taking people out on angling trips became the business.'

After getting a degree in marine biology and a long spell working for the fisheries, Carl came back to carry on the family tradition. If anyone has ordered a lobster at Paysanne, chances are that it was Carl who hauled the beast up from the deep.

Most of his pots are scattered around the Great Orme in Llandudno, where the crab is especially well regarded. 'We get them from round the Orme and further offshore once they start to move about a bit. They are a smaller crab than you tend to get down south, and generally a smaller crab, for whatever reason, has a higher meat content.'

Lobster is, it goes without saying, one of the very great delicacies – the first thing that springs to mind when you have an anniversary or a special birthday looming over the horizon. Carl is very aware of the special nature of his catch, as well as the importance of maintaining stocks and not over-fishing. 'In June, the lobsters are moulting and mating, and when their eggs are hatching they're not particularly interested in going into the pots, but come mid-June there'll be a feeding frenzy and you'll catch a lot of them who've only just shed their shell. These go straight back in the water – we end up putting back about a third of what we catch.'

This may be 'high days and holidays' fare, but so what? We've all had a weird few years. No one will begrudge you a little spoil…

CRAB CAKES WITH WATERCRESS AND CURRIED MAYONNAISE

CRAB CAKES WITH WATERCRESS AND CURRIED MAYONNAISE

Ingredients for the crab cakes:

600g crab meat (white and brown)

300g mashed potatoes

4 spring onions, finely chopped

½ tsp cayenne pepper

½ bunch chives, chopped

5g Dijon mustard

1 egg, beaten

Method:

- Mix all the ingredients together and shape into equally sized cakes.

- Refrigerate for 1 hour to allow them to firm up.

- Remove from the fridge and dust with flour.

- Warm a frying pan and shallow fry the crab cakes for 5-6 minutes on each side (don't try and move them or turn them until they've started to develop a crust).

Ingredients for the curried mayonnaise:

80g mayonnaise

40g easy curry paste

10g coriander, chopped

1 lime, juice only

- Combine all of the ingredients and serve

Method:

- Combine all of the ingredients and serve.

'The Great Orme is about 500 yards from where I work. It's famous for the goats that took over Llandudno and made headlines worldwide during the pandemic – they're still in town now, munching on the occasional privet hedge. However, the Great Orme crabs definitely deserve a mention too.'

Toby Watson

CRAB COCKTAIL, BLOODY MARY MAYONNAISE AND CRAB TOASTS

CRAB COCKTAIL, BLOODY MARY MAYONNAISE AND CRAB TOASTS

Ingredients:

300g white crab meat

100g brown crab meat

1 fennel bulb, finely sliced

1 orange, segmented

1 lemon, juice only

1 small bunch chives, chopped

1 small bunch dill, chopped

4 slices wholegrain bread

1 avocado, thinly sliced

Olive oil

2 gem lettuces, chopped into quarters

Method:

- Mix the sliced fennel with the orange, lemon juice and a pinch of salt and set aside for 1 hour.

- Mix the crab with the chopped dill. Add the sliced avocado to the fennel salad and assemble the cocktails by layering the lettuce, salad mix and crab throughout.

- Top with the Bloody Mary mayonnaise and serve with toasted wholemeal bread spread with the brown crab meat and topped with chives.

Ingredients for Bloody Mary mayonnaise:

80g mayonnaise

80g ketchup

½ tsp Worcestershire sauce

5 drops Tabasco

5ml vodka

Pinch celery salt

1 lemon, juice only

Method:

- Combine all of the ingredients and serve.

'The quintessential British prawn cocktail is everyone's nan's favourite, but this really takes it up a gear. I love the punch of a bloody Mary against the silky sweetness of the crab.'
Toby Watson

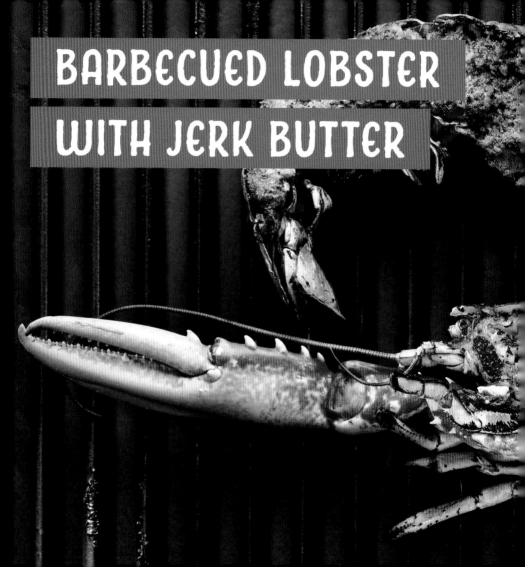

BARBECUED LOBSTER WITH JERK BUTTER

BARBECUED LOBSTER WITH JERK BUTTER

Ingredients:

2 x 750g cooked lobsters

25g garlic

25g ginger

3 spring onions

2g coriander seeds

2g fennel seeds

2g black pepper

40g white wine vinegar

40g soy sauce

120g butter

1 lemon, juice and zest

¼ bunch thyme, chopped

½ chilli, deseeded

4 lemon wedges

Method:

- Split the lobster in half lengthways and place on a baking tray.

- Toast the coriander seeds and fennel seeds in a dry pan for 2 minutes, then grind them with a pestle and mortar.

- Place all the remaining ingredients into a mixer and blitz. Combine the two and set aside.

- Brush the lobster flesh with a little oil and place them on a roaring barbecue for 2 minutes, then turn them over so that the shell is face down.

- Spoon the butter mix wherever you can over the lobster and cook for a further 5 minutes. Season with salt and serve with a lemon wedge.

LOBSTER AND NDUJA
FLATBREAD PIZZA

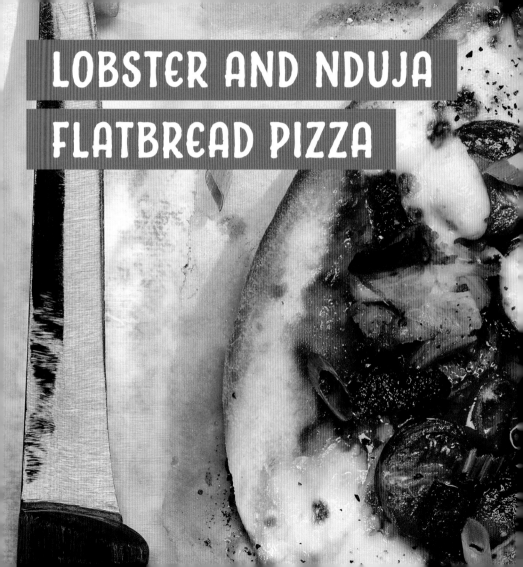

LOBSTER AND NDUJA FLATBREAD PIZZA

Ingredients:

2 cooked lobsters, meat chopped up

100g nduja paste (or chorizo if you can't get it)

24 cherry tomatoes, halved

4 spring onions, thinly sliced

2 red chillies, thinly sliced and deseeded

80ml soured cream

50g pizza mozzarella, diced

100g butter, room temperature

8 cloves garlic, crushed

140ml warm water

½ tsp dried yeast

5g sugar

2g salt

100g Greek yoghurt

¼ tsp smoked paprika

400g flour

Vegetable oil

Method:

- First, make the flatbreads by adding the yeast to the warm water and sugar and leaving for 5 minutes.

- Pour the liquid onto the flour, paprika and salt and mix together. Next, add the Greek yoghurt and combine to a dough.

- Knead the dough for 5 minutes until smooth, then split the mix into four and set aside for an hour or until it has almost doubled in size.

- Roll out the dough, using extra flour if necessary, and fry them in a pan with a touch of olive oil for 2-3 minutes on each side.

- In a bowl, combine the garlic and butter. Spread this over the flatbreads and top with nduja, cherry tomatoes, red chilli, diced mozzarella and lobster.

- Bake in the oven for 6 minutes. Remove and top with the spring onion and soured cream. Season with salt and pepper.

'I'm not a lover of surf and turf, but the spice on the nduja and the bleed of the oil really works well with the sweetness of the lobster.'
Toby Watson

FISHELLANEOUS

There are plenty of fish in the sea. This isn't just sage, if uninspired, dating advice – there's all manner of fish and seafood out there along the coast of North Wales and beyond, far too many for us to cram into this one book. However, in the interests of variety, here are some extra recipes from Toby's repertoire to provide a final flourish of fishy finesse. Actually, the first one is swiped from my mum's notepad of inspiration when she was putting the first Paysanne menu together in 1988.

PAYSANNE SOUPE DE PÊCHEUR

Paysanne Soupe de Pêcheur

Ingredients:

250ml fish stock

900g chopped, mixed fish fillets (something sturdy like coley, monkfish or grey mullet; sea bass, for example, would just dissolve. The French use things like dogfish, gurnard or rockfish)

1 leek

1 onion

1 bulb fennel

2 sticks celery

1 red pepper

1 red chilli

3 tbsp of good olive oil

Half an orange, zest only

Pastis (a healthy glug)

2 large cloves garlic, crushed

Handful chopped basil

1 sachet saffron

1 tin chopped tomatoes

1 dsp tomato purée

Salt and pepper

Method:

- Bring the fish stock to a boil, then keep on a low heat while you prep the rest of the ingredients.

- Chop up all the vegetables, finely chop the chilli and fry them all on a low heat together with the garlic in olive oil for 10 minutes until everything is soft and golden.

- Add the chopped tomatoes, tomato purée and basil. Using your biggest ladle, carefully spoon the hot stock over the vegetables and stir.

- Take a deep breath, forget about the expense and empty the sachet of saffron into the pot! Give the whole thing several twists of salt and pepper, bring to the boil, then drop the heat and simmer for about 30 minutes.

- Add the fish, orange zest and a healthy splash of Pastis (Ricard if you can get it). Leave to simmer for another 15 minutes.

- If you want to transform this into a full-on feast, add some sliced new potatoes and king prawns at the fish-adding stage. Serve with toasted croûtes and some homemade aïoli.

'This is a Bouillabaisse-style recipe that has served us well at Paysanne for over 30 years. My mum was making it in 1988, and this is a slight variation on the recipe still used today by Paysanne's chef, David Hughes.'
Cai Ross

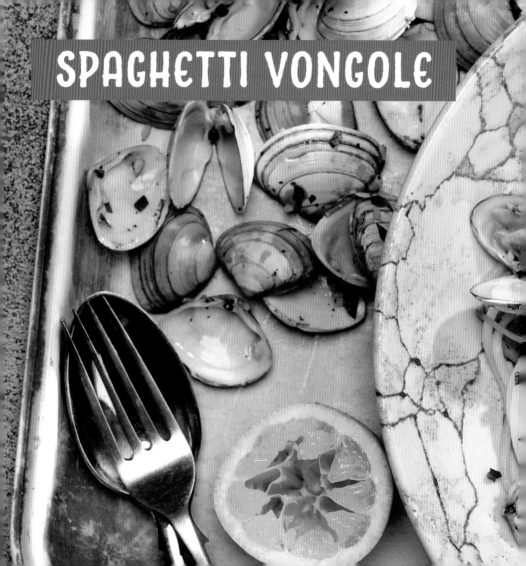

SPAGHETTI VONGOLE

SPAGHETTI VONGOLE

Ingredients:

1kg clams

350g fresh spaghetti

5 tbsp olive oil

4 cloves garlic, crushed

½ red chilli, deseeded and finely diced

100ml white wine

1 bunch flat-leaf parsley, chopped

1 lemon, juice only

Method:

- Clean the clams by soaking them in salty water for about 30 minutes, then sit them in unsalted cold water for a further 10 minutes – this should allow them to release any sand and grit.

- Cook the spaghetti in boiling water to *al dente*.

- Heat the olive oil in a sauté pan and add the chilli and garlic. Cook for a couple of minutes but do not colour.

- Add the clams to the pan with the white wine, turn up to full heat and shake.

- Cook for 2-3 minutes until the clams open (discard any that don't).

- Throw in your drained pasta (don't worry if it still has a bit of starchy water on it).

- Finally, finish with the chopped parsley and a squeeze of lemon, salt and black pepper.

GRILLED SARDINES WITH TOMATOES, BREAD AND SALSA VERDE

GRILLED SARDINES WITH TOMATOES, BREAD AND SALSA VERDE

Ingredients:

8 plum tomatoes, thinly sliced

½ red onion, finely sliced

1 tbsp extra virgin olive oil

1 tsp sugar

20 sardine fillets

1 bunch basil, torn

½ bunch tarragon

½ bunch flat-leaf parsley

50ml olive oil

4 salted anchovies

4 cloves garlic, crushed

20ml red wine vinegar

30g capers

¼ ciabatta, charred with olive oil and torn into chunks

Method:

- Place half the basil, the tarragon, parsley, olive oil, two-thirds of the garlic, anchovies, red wine vinegar and half of the capers in a food processor and blitz to a paste.

- Mix the tomatoes with the remaining capers, garlic, basil, red onions, sugar and a generous glug of good extra virgin olive oil. Season with salt and black pepper.

- Leave for 20 minutes, then lay out on a platter layering through the bread just before serving.

- Meanwhile, rub some sea salt liberally over the sardines and place under a hot grill for 5 minutes. Top with lashings of the salsa verde.

'Tinned sardines with tomato sauce on toast are a memory of my childhood. If only my mum had known how to make salsa verde.'
Toby Watson

'When I was a kid, a big treat was going to Siop Nain in Ruthin to eat sardine and mustard toasties, which at the time felt like James Bond-level elegance and refinement. I still make them now.'
Cai Ross

STOCKS AND
SAUCES

We live, sadly, in the age of the microwaveable packet sauce. All sorts of easy options are out there to help you shave some time off your prep, but we urge you to stand firm and treat your seafood dish to the dignity of a sauce made freshly and lovingly with your own hands. Here are a few examples that are all easy to make and will give such a lift to your fishy dishy.

All you need is a little patience and the certainty that your dinner guests will be gushing superlatives all the way to the cheese course.

TARTARE SAUCE

Ingredients:

140g mayonnaise

1 lemon, juice only

1 shallot, finely chopped

30g capers

30g gherkins, chopped

1 tbsp flat-leaf parsley, chopped

Method:

• Combine all the ingredients. That's it!

'I've often heard it said that the difference between food being plain fuel and being a meal is the sauce. Fernand Point said, "In the orchestra of a great kitchen, the sauce chef is a soloist", and who are we to argue with one of the greatest chefs of all time?'
Cai Ross

BÉARNAISE SAUCE

Ingredients:

200g unsalted butter

2 shallots, finely chopped

Pinch black pepper

1 clove garlic, crushed

2 egg yolks

50ml white wine vinegar

2 tbsp chopped tarragon

Method:

- Melt the butter in a saucepan and leave to one side to allow the clarified butter and solids to separate (you'll only use the clear butter on top).

- Place the shallots, pepper, garlic and vinegar in a pan and reduce the liquid by half.

- Leave to cool, then place this mix along with the egg yolks and 30ml of cold water into a mixer.

- Give it a quick whizz, then turn the mixer to its lowest setting. Slowly pour in the clarified butter and watch the sauce emulsify.

- Once it has thickened, remove the sauce from the blender, season it and stir through the tarragon.

CHILLI DIPPING SAUCE

Ingredients:

50g garlic, crushed

100g red pepper, finely chopped

250g sugar

200ml rice vinegar

25g dried chilli flakes

50g red chilli, deseeded and chopped

80g fish sauce

Method:

- Place the garlic, red pepper, sugar, rice vinegar, chilli flakes, and chillies in a pan and bring to a simmer.

- Immediately remove from the heat and allow to cool.

- Stir in the fish sauce and serve.

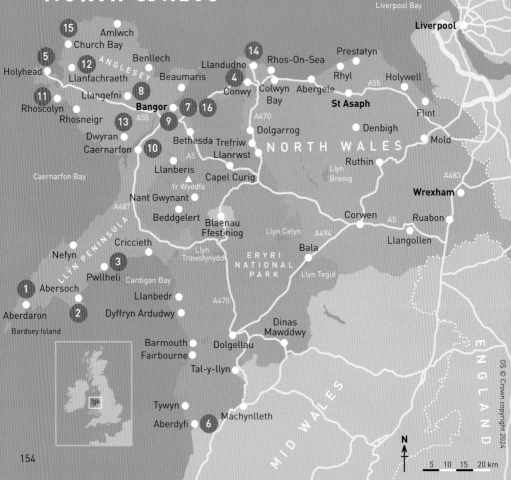

NORTH WALES

NORTH WALES SEAFOOD SUPPLIERS AND WHOLESALERS

 Retail   **Wholesale**   **Export**

1. Aberdaron Seafood
Natalie Harrison
Pendref, Aberdaron
Pwllheli, Gwynedd LL53 8BG
t: 07800 574689
e: natalieaberdaron@gmail.com
Fresh, hand-picked crab.

2. Bwyd Môr Abersoch Seafood
Annwen Jones
Henryd, Sarn Bach, Abersoch
Gwynedd LL53 7DA
t: 01758 712005
e: bmabersoch@outlook.com
Crab and Lobster, live or dressed, available
March to December.

3. Bwyd O'r Mor/
Pwllheli Seafood's Ltd
Richard Evans
Outer Harbour, Pwllheli
Gwynedd LL53 5AY
t: 01758 614615
e: sales@bwydormor.co.uk
w: www.bwydormor.co.uk
Fresh shellfish and wet fish, available all year
round.

4. Conwy Mussels
Thomas Jones
The Quay, Conwy LL32 8BB
t: 01492 592689
e: info@conwymussels.com
w: www.conwymussels.com
Hand-raked Conwy mussels, available
September-April, plus fresh fish counter.

5. D A Wood Shellfish
David Wood
Tŷ Croes, Llanfaethlu, Holyhead,
Isle of Anglesey LL65 4PE
t: 07860 752802
e: Dwoodshellfish@aol.com
Brown crab and lobster.

6. Dai's Shed
David Hughes
Fishermen's Unit, Canolfan Dyfi,
Aberdyfi, Gwynedd LL35 0EE
t: 07944 264821
e: gill@gillyfish.co.uk
w: www.daisshed.co.uk
Seasonal fish and shellfish.

7. Deep Dock Mussels Ltd
James Wilson
Port Penrhyn, Bangor,
Gwynedd LL57 4HN
t: 01248 354878
e: info@menaimusselmen.com
w: www.menaimusselmen.com
Fresh, live Menai mussels, available all year
round.

8. Extra Mussel Ltd
Trevor Jones
Refail, Llanffinan, Llangefni,
Isle of Anglesey LL77 7SN
t: 01248 722969
e: trevormussels@yahoo.com
w: www.menaimusselmen.com
Fresh, live Menai Mussels, available all year
round.

9. Fish on Line
(Môn Shellfish Ltd)
Mark Gray
Unit 1, Intec, Ffordd y Parc,
Parc Menai, Bangor, Gwynedd LL57 4FG
t: 07476 300930
e: mark.bwyd.mor@gmail.com
w: www.fishonline.wales/
Locally sourced shellfish and fin fish, sold to
to local restaurants and direct to the public.

10. H J Heard Hughes
Mike Hughes
68 Pool Street, Caernarfon,
Gwynedd LL55 2AF
t: 01286 672672
e: sales@jhearvdhughes.co.uk
Local fish and shellfish supplier.

11. Holy Island Seafood
Tracy Jones
Beach Road, Llainysbylldir, Rhoscolyn
Isle of Anglesey LL65 2NJ
t: 01407 861699
e: holyislandseafood@hotmail.co.uk
w: www.holyislandseafood.co.uk
Crab, lobster, scallops and ready meals, all
subject to availability, open all year round.

12. MJ White Fishmongers
Mathew White
15 Parc Llynnon, Valley
Isle of Anglesey LL65 4DL
t: 07827 415883
e: mattfish7628@googlemail.com
w: www.mjwhitefishmongers.co.uk
Mobile fishmonger, with fresh fish and
shellfish sourced locally.

13. Menai Oysters and Mussels
Shaun Krijnen
Tal Y Bont Bach, Dwyran, Llanfairpwll
Isle of Anglesey LL61 6UU
t: 01248 430878
e: theoysterman@btopenworld.com
w: www.menaioysters.co.uk
Oysters and Mussels harvested from the
Menai Strait, available on Sundays and
Wednesdays.

14. Mermaid Seafoods
Sonya Jones
Builder Street, Llandudno,
Conwy LL30 1DR
t: 01492 878014
e: enquiries@mermaidseafoods.co.uk
w: www.mermaidseafoods.co.uk
High-quality fish and shellfish, available all
year.

15. Môn Dressed Crab
Tracy Hodson
Church Bay, Isle of Anglesey LL65 4EU
t: 07761 368858 / 01407 730170
e: tlhod69@gmail.com
Locally sourced dressed crab.

16. Myti Mussels Ltd
Kim Mould
Porth Penrhyn, Bangor
Gwynedd LL57 4HN
t: 01248 354878
e: kimmussels@hotmail.com
w: www.menaimusselmen.com
Fresh, live Menai mussels, available all year
round.

METRIC AND IMPERIAL EQUIVALENTS

Weights	Solid		Volume	Liquid
15g	½oz		15ml	½ fl oz
25g	1oz		30ml	1 fl oz
40g	1½oz		50ml	2 fl oz
50g	1¾oz		100ml	3½ fl oz
75g	2¾oz		125ml	4 fl oz
100g	3½oz		150ml	5 fl oz (¼ pint)
125g	4½oz		200ml	7 fl oz
150g	5½oz		250ml	9 fl oz
175g	6oz		300ml	10 fl oz (½ pint)
200g	7oz		400ml	14 fl oz
250g	9oz		450ml	16 fl oz
300g	10½oz		500ml	18 fl oz
400g	14oz		600ml	1 pint (20 fl oz)
500g	1lb 2oz		1 litre	1¾ pints
1kg	2lb 4oz		1.2 litre	2 pints
1.5kg	3lb 5oz		1.5 litre	2¾ pints
2kg	4lb 8oz		2 litres	3½ pints
3kg	6lb 8oz		3 litres	5¼ pints

THANKS

Thank you so much to the following for helping us with this book: Colin and Charlotte Bennett, Carl Davies, Tom Jones, Shaun Krijnen, Alison Lea-Wilson, Charles Meadows and Danny White-Meir. Thanks to all our fantastic local suppliers in North Wales, particularly Mermaid Seafoods in Llandudno. Thanks from Cai to David Hughes and all the amazing staff at Paysanne. Thanks from Toby to everyone at Outside for their tireless work.

Finally, thanks to Liss, Caitlin and Hugo, to Sarah, Ivy and Mavis, and to everyone at Graffeg Publishing for a wonderful book.

North Wales: Fish & Seafood
Published in Great Britain in 2024 by
Graffeg Limited.

Written by Cai Ross and Toby Watson © 2024.
Food photography by Huw Jones © 2024.
Food styling by Andre Moore.
Post-production by Matt Braham.
Designed and produced by Graffeg Limited
© 2024.

Graffeg Limited, 24 Stradey Park Business
Centre, Mwrwg Road, Llangennech, Llanelli,
Carmarthenshire, SA14 8YP, Wales, UK.
Tel: 01554 824000. www.graffeg.com.

Cai Ross and Toby Watson are hereby identified as
the authors of this work in accordance with section
77 of the Copyright, Designs and Patents Act 1988.

A CIP Catalogue record for this book is available
from the British Library.

The publisher gratefully acknowledges the
financial support of this book by the Books Council
of Wales. www.gwales.com.

ISBN 9781802585377

1 2 3 4 5 6 7 8 9

Photography: © Conwy Borough Council:
End paper – page 1. All other photography
© Huw Jones.

North Wales:
Fish & Seafood